7 Essentials for

Tapping into the Veins of God

Finding the Flow of God's Anointing for Your Life

Bishop Jeffrey L. Melvin

DEDICATION

I dedicate this my first book to my Lord, my Savior Jesus who is the Christ.

I am crucified with Christ: nevertheless, I live; yet not I, but Christ liveth in me: and the life which I now live in the flesh I live by the faith of the Son of God, Who loved me, and gave himself for me.

(Galatians 2:20-21)

CONTENTS

ACKNOWLEDGMENTS

My wife since 1982, Queen Dee the Queen Bee. Deborah Denise Melvin, love you to life, girl.

Special thank you my Sister Minister Kimberly Young, also to Mother Barbara Price. Thank you both for wrestling with my very challenging writing and spelling style.

To all the beautiful saints of the *Power House & Encouragement Centre Churches of God in Christ* and along with my beautiful jurisdiction of Rwanda East Africa, thank you for your unwavering love and continued support.

To my mother-in-*love* Missionary Wyreen Jones and our church mother, Mother Janice Monroe, thank you for your love and care of me.

To Leanora Driggs thank you for that fateful call that connected me to Ebony Nicole.

To my publisher, Sis. Ebony Nicole Smith, you are the glue that bound this book together. Get ready to blow up!

.

i

WHERE BE THE MIRACLES?

"And Gideon said unto him, Oh my Lord, if the LORD be with us, why then is all this befallen us? Where be all his miracles which our fathers told us of, saying, 'Did not the LORD bring us up from Egypt?' But now the LORD hath forsaken us and delivered us into the hands of the Midianites."
(Judges 6:13)

The Strong Memorial hospital is one of the most renown and prestigious hospitals on the east coast. It is the teaching hospital of another institution of renown, the University of Rochester. The U of R is a coveted University that boasts of being a place where patients abound, research is fluid and medical doctors and scientists are produced yearly.

It was at Strong Memorial hospital where I once again found myself attending to a member that had suddenly fallen ill. Being a full time Pastor, this was not only a part

1

of my calling, it was also a part of my job. No problem, because I love people and I'm working in my dream occupation while abiding in my calling. When I arrived, Sister Audrey Alexander was yet in the waiting room. She had been waiting for over an hour and was complaining of chest pains and numbness in her left arm. The sister that was there with her told me what was happening, and I was not happy at all, to say the least. I immediately went to the intake person who was casually perched at her desk and said,

"Young lady I am not a doctor, I am a pastor. However, I think when a female patient is complaining of chest pains, numbness down her arm, not to mention a severe headache, it should be reason for acute concern. Wouldn't you say so?"

She replied, "Well, Pastor, I am not a doctor myself, but I will make sure that she is seen next."

Soon, Sister Alexander was whisked back to the triage area of the emergency department. Within minutes a young man wearing a bright yellow shirt entered the room.

"Miss. Alexander, I need to draw some blood from you."

She replied, "OK but my veins are a little hard to find."

He assured her, "I will do my best." The young man tied off her arm with the tourniquet, then tapped her inner arm and proceeded to poke her with a needle, looking for the vein.

I could tell just by looking at him that he was a novice. You see, I come from a family of nurses. My mom was a nurse, my two sisters are nurses. I have at least six cousins in nursing, not to mention three aunts and even an uncle. I even successfully completed six weeks of medical training in order to work as a mental health treatment aide for the State of New York. Although my training did not involve drawing blood, we worked closely with both L.P.N. (Licensed Practical Nurses) and RNs (Registered Nurses). You may ask, does that quality me to say this guy was a novice? No, but the fact that the vein did not even pop up in her arm does. This guy was just poking and poking and when he couldn't find the vein, he summoned another *yellow shirt*. A young lady came in, and as you can imagine, she too, poked and missed, and poked and missed.

Finally, I told Sister Alexander, "Listen, my younger sister Tonda worked here as a dialysis nurse years ago. She told me that if you keep poking at the vein and missing, that you can have what they call a collapsed vein. That is similar to having a blowout on car tire. Once that happens you can never use that vein again to draw blood, ever!! We better get a doctor or a phlebotomist. I'm not sure who these *yellow shirt* folks are, but they don't seem to know how to get your veins to pop up."

Sister Alexander agreed and when the next person came into the room she told her, "I am tired of being poked and stuck by people who can't find my veins. I admit that my veins are small and elusive, but I demand a specialist."

This time the young lady said, "Miss I have just the person." In a few short minutes, in popped a middle-aged Registered Nurse. She announced her name and said, "I am here to tap that tricky vein of yours!" Now from the start I liked this nurse, she was confident, smiling and cheery, her enthusiasm lit up the room. Even with all of that I said we were still skeptical.

"I am glad that you feel that you can find Miss. Alexander's vein, but what makes you so sure of yourself? She has been being poked to no avail for about 30 minutes?"

She answered, "Pastor, I am the specialist around here. They call me when all else fails. Besides, these folks in the *yellow shirts* (she whispered), are nurse trainees. They were just practicing. But please don't tell anybody that I told you that." She then methodically and precisely began to tie off the middle of Sister Alexander's arm. I noticed that she used two tourniquets instead of one. Then she slapped her arm so hard that it left a mark, but suddenly there appeared a big ole' vein. Even I could have tapped that vein with ease! We all looked in astonishment as she took tube after tube of blood. She then called one of the *yellow shirts* back into the room to send the blood to the lab for testing.

As she began to leave, and we were all just staring in astonishment, I said, "Please, wait. Before you leave, tell me why it was so easy for you to tap into the vein."

She responded, with the same big grin, "First of all, I'm good, and I got good by doing what I do for a long time. Secondly, I always use two tourniquets. You must put pressure on the arm to cut off the flow so that the blood builds up will be prominent and the vein will stick up. Lastly, I always believe that I'm going to hit the vein every time. That way I keep my title as this hospital's *vein specialist.*"

Boy you should have seen me, the Bishop, world traveler and prophet, with my mouth dropped open. She spun on her heels and walked out of the door. Sister

Alexander said, "Pastor, are you alright?"

I acknowledged her question, "Yes, I'm fine, but God just dropped a book into my spirit 'Tapping into the vein of God."

She laughed, but I was totally serious.

VEIN TAPPERS

Imagine if we all had the expertise that the nurse had. I wish that I had gotten her name, but I didn't. She affected my life in a profound way. Like I said before, she was confident. That word comes from two words in the Greek, *"Con"* meaning foreword and *"Fidelity"* meaning strength. So, to be confident is to have "foreword strength," the strength to go in the knowledge that even before you begin, the job is done.

I want to explore just how the believer can tap into the strength, anointing, promise, healing and everything else that God has promised us.

She, the nurse, was experienced.

Remember the *yellow shirt* folks? Well they were merely students. Since Strong Memorial is a teaching hospital they had to get their practice from somewhere. I just didn't want them practicing on Sister Alexander. I sure don't want them practicing on me! By the way, Sister Alexander came out alright and today she is healthy and doing fine.

That nurse had been in her profession long enough to learn some tricks of the trade. She took the same tubing that the rookies used to tie off the blood flow, but if you recall she used two, to put extra pressure on her arm. When I ask her why, she said, "I always use two for the hard cases." You see, some things are 'hard cases' in our lives and it is going to take some extra pressure on our knees, in our study time and in the crucifixion of our flesh. She also could feel in the crease of the arm and know that there was indeed a good vein there. It was not blown, just hidden. You have to know when your blessing is not gone, just unattained, just lying dormant. She did not see it but she knew that is was there. Her nursing experience, confidence and her training lead her to believe that she would strike gold every time.

Can you hear me shouting, Halleluiah! as I am writing this paragraph?!

My God, she was the specialist alright. She knew how to put her patient at ease and then back up her talking with evidence. You know a lot of people do a lot of talking but where is the evidence? In my heart I am crying out:

GOD, WE NEED SOME EVIDENCE OF YOUR VEIN BEING ALIVE AND NOT BLOWN.

She had the faith that she would not disappoint her

hospital, patient or even herself. "I plan to hit the vein every time," she said.

Lord, we need to hit Your vein every time, each and every time; praise God!

Let's go a little further...

In our Scriptural text, Judges 6, we find a scary fella named Gideon. Let me give you a little background on him. His name means, "hewn down or cut off." He is what we might call 'shell shocked,' which is derived from times at war when the soldier would hear continuous bombings – many landings very close to them, while others had taken the lives of their comrades in battle. After time, just the anticipation of a bomb dropping would make that 'shell shocked' soldier just about lose his lunch, one way or the other, if you know what I mean.

Now, the Israelites had fallen in love with foreign gods. They left the commandment of the only true God that said, "*Ye shall have no other gods before me (Exodus 20:3)*", and they went a whoring after the gods. For this cause, God was forced to turn them over to the gods that they had fallen in love with. You see, God hates to have to discipline us, nor does He take pleasure in our chastisement, but in order to be true to His word He cannot look on sin with approval. Not only that, God in His infinite wisdom knows that the chastisement of the Lord brings forth the peaceable fruits of righteousness (Hebrews 12:11). He only allows our enemies to appear triumphant to show us that He is the only true God. In fact, Jesus said that He is the way the truth and the life.

Gideon, along with the rest of Israel, would plant seed during sowing season and irrigate their crops and hire workers to help harvest the fields during reaping season. They had taken all of that time, effort and hard labor into their work only to have the Midianites wait until the peak of the reaping time and come sweep down to take what they had labored for all season long. They took everything of value - the crops, the goats, the sheep, why I am sure that they even took the family dog named Spot! They had no pity on these folks, none. So, because of their fright, the Israelites resorted to hiding the spoils in dens and caves or wherever they could in order to just have food to eat and clothes to wear. And these were the people of God, the Hebrews, the anointed of the Lord.

"And the angel of the Lord appeared unto him and said unto him: the Lord is with thee, thou mighty man of valor."
(Judges 6:12)

Let me explain that it is commonly accepted by Bible scholars that the angel of the Lord is indeed Jesus in the spirit realm or the pre-incarnate Jesus. It is utterly amazing that God Himself would think enough not only of Israel, but also of Gideon, that He would appear unto Gideon bodily. Notice how The Lord saluted Gideon, "The Lord is with thee, thou mighty man of valor." It was customary to greet folks during that time by their title or their perceived status. They would use such greetings as, "God be with you, my Sister," or "Greetings, my Lord (Mister)," or "Man of God." In this particular greeting, the Lord's salutation to Gideon appeared to be off base. He referred to him as a "Mighty Man of Valor." This completely blew Gideon's mind. He must have wondered just who he was talking to. Listen to his response: "If we be such a great group of people, where are the promises?" Well, have you ever felt like that?

> *OK God. I have received prophecy, after prophecy, after prophecy...I felt that they were indeed accurate. However, they have yet to come to pass. Where are the miracles? And how can you refer to me as Mighty and a Man of valor, when I am among a scary, trifling, shaky, beaten down people? A people that are running from folks that should be running from them! Not to mention the fact that I am a chump too!!*

Here in lies the real dilemma:

> Others are prospering like a green bay tree, and they don't love God the way that you do, but every time you look up they are receiving blessing, after blessing, after blessing (see Psalms 73). Maybe they have received new car, a new house, a new job, or better yet, they seem to have it all together. They are at peace; their children

are the most well-behaved, scholar athletes in the school. And yours? Well Tyrone was diagnosed with ADD, Tyresha just told you that she was pregnant, Timecka feels that she is as grown as you and Tydooka just came from Planned Parenthood with some bad news. The car is running so badly that you are often late for work, but the car note arrives right on time every month (and by the way the payment is late again this month).

You are having to work a second job under the table because the bills, the bill collectors and the IRS are after you. Also, the rent lady is stalking you. The phone has an old message from the Pastor, wondering why you have been missing so much church. You have not paid the Lord His tithes since God knows when. All the while the people around you, the sinners, your unsaved loved ones, the hustlers, drug dealers and those that have sugar daddies and friends with benefits, seem to be doing just fine. And you are screaming out, "Lord, where are the promises?"

By the way, that was my modern-day rendition of brother Gideon's situation. You see, there is nothing new under the sun. Challenges are common to man. What we need to explore at this point is just how this issue was dealt with by God, through brother Gideon.

I believe that God is immutable, that is to say unchangeable. If He cared for His people back in the day, then He cares for His people today. If He wanted His people blessed back in the day, He wants them blessed today. I also believe that it is up to us to begin tapping into God, to arouse in Him the reality that we do want to live better, walk better, and produce better, to bring glory to Him and be a blessing to those around us.

God refers to us in the prophetic

"And the angel of the Lord appeared unto him, and said unto him, the Lord is with thee thou mighty man of valor."
(Judges 6:12)

Let's once again look at this all-important verse. First off, the Lord appeared unto him. This lets us know that God himself saw something not only in Gideon, but also in the time, space, and reason for his showing himself to Gideon now. In other words, our 'right now' is what puts a necessary demand on our situation.

I can remember the pain of my past, however, the mess that I am in now makes my yesterday hurt less. Gideon and Israel had a 'right now' problem. Obviously, God heard the cries of the Hebrews and came to give them help. I am glad that we serve a God that will show up when we need Him. However, it is important for <u>you</u> to know that He will show up when <u>you</u> call him.

David said, *"This poor man cried, and the Lord inclined onto me."* (Psalm 34:6)

James said, *"You have not because you ask not."* (James 4:2)

Israel was in pain and God responded to the painful cries of his people.

I remember as a child that my mother, (who was a single parent for most of her life), would sometimes give me a good old fashioned behind whooping for some mischief that I had gotten into. Back then, I got into a lot. One day I told my sister Kim, "I think I am getting too old for mommy to be spanking me. The next time she calls herself spanking me I'm not going to cry."

Kim said, "I wouldn't do that if I was you, Jeff."

I replied, "Just watch and see, I refuse to cry again." Well as providence would have it I did something stupid and it was whooping time. As was her custom, Mom demanded,

"Pull down those pants. I can't afford to wear out those good jeans. I want your backside." She commenced to whipping me with one of those long switches that I had to hand pick from the backyard. (Mind you part of the humiliation of the punishment was that you had to go into the yard and pick your own switch, and it had to meet with Mom's specifications of a 'good switch'.) I bit down hard on my lip trying to bear the pain. Mom had a firm grip on my wrist. I danced around making muffled whimpering sounds like a wounded pet, but I refused to cry. I had it in my mind that I was going to be a man and not give her the satisfaction of seeing tears or hearing screams. When Mom caught on to my ploy, she got as hot as a pistol and said to me, as my three sisters peeked around the corner watching the show,

"Oh, I guess you think that you are too grown to make me think that this whopping is doing you any good huh?" Right then she put her motions in super over-drive and gave me the beat down of my life. Boy I began to jump and cry and scream and plead for mercy.

"Momma, I'm sorry! I promise that I will never do it again, I promise!!!" I was just like James Brown screaming 'Please, Please, Please, Please!' She put it on me so badly that she could not hear my sisters laughing over all of my loud crying. I learned a valuable lesson that day. If you are in pain, you had better cry out to someone who can do something about it. By the way, I had the greatest mother in the world. I deserved and thanked her for every spanking she ever gave me. They helped me to be the man that I am today.

Back to Gideon...
God Appeared unto them because He heard their cries. The Lord then declared that He was with them.
"The Lord is with thee."
(Judges 6:12)

Is there a greater comfort to have in all the world than to know that the Lord is with you? That word from the angel of the Lord should have said it all. However, Gideon would need some convincing. In fact, he'd need a lot of convincing.

The Lord then proclaimed who their deliverer and leader would be. He said to Gideon, "Thou Mighty Man of Valor." Once again this is a prophetic proclamation over Gideon life. Gideon was fully aware that this particular greeting referred to a brave man of war.

Notice that GIDEON DID NOT EVEN RESPOND TO WHAT WAS SAID ABOUT HIM. RATHER HE WENT RIGHT TO THE DELIMMA IN WHICH HIS COUNTRY WAS INVOLVED.

To me, it seemed like Gideon could not conceive of being any type of conquer or redeemer based upon the shaky condition of Israel. It would be like an angel telling you that you would bring your family out of the grips of poverty, welfare, alcoholism, and crack addiction, when all the while you know that this has been the family mantra for over forty years. *Mom had six babies, six baby-daddies. Father was lost and turned out, hasn't been seen since you were in diapers. Siblings have been in jail, prison, on the streets, drug users and drug abusers.* Then there is the other side. *Maybe you are a Christian, God loving, God fearing. You are in church every Sunday, a frequent giver, you don't cuss, don't chew gum in church, don't even think about going to the club. But you are living with a systemic legacy of poverty, sickness and frustration.* In both of these cases you need to be able to hear those words *"Mighty Man"* or *"Mighty Woman."*

My wife of over thirty years, Deborah Denise Melvin, once told me of a story from her youth. She said that when she was a little girl, she gave her parents so much trouble that they did not know what to do with her. This child had a furious fighting spirit. I'm told that she actually loved to fight anywhere, anyhow, anytime. She would climb on top of the refrigerator and jump across the kitchen like she was a super heroine or something. Now, if you ever met Deborah, you would not believe that she could be the terror that she was. Her parents, although loving and giving, needed help with this here child. So, in stepped Grandma Roena. Grandma was a wise mother who loved the Lord. She lived in Opelika, Alabama. At the time my wife's family lived at the place of her birth. A place called Brick Quarters in Orlando Florida. Well, they drove over 500 miles to Opelika to see if Grandma could help with this child. As the story is told by my wife, the main thing that grandma did was to proclaim to Deborah that she was a 'good girl.' She would say, "There goes my good girl," or "Here is grandma's good girl."

Deborah told me, "Grandma knew that I was bad, but she spoke into my life. She spoke it until I started acting good." A few years later at a very young age, my wife-to-be received Jesus as her Lord and Savior. She was baptized in the Holy Ghost and is now a Bishop's wife. Thank God that grandma had the God-given wisdom to speak life into her life. I am all the more blessed because of Grandma's proclamation. And as a tribute to her grandmother, Deborah now speaks to some of our more challenged nieces and nephews (over one-hundred in all). "You are such a good boy." or "Here comes Aunt Deborah's good girl." They may know that they have a family reputation of being the black sheep, but when they see her coming they straighten right up and act like they are good.

That is what Jesus was trying to instill into the heart of Gideon. "You are Mighty, you are Brave, you are Valiant." And I tell you today, if God said it, then it is already so. It does not matter in what form the Word comes. Whether by reading it in the Bible, or through a prophetic utterance, or even through a grandparent, we must learn to grab hold to any Word that would give us that motivation or that spirit of encouragement to catapult us to a brand-new day.

Just grab it...grab it...NOW!!

GIDEON'S CHALLENGE

Thank God for the patient nature of God. He already knew that Gideon would not immediately walk in agreement with His words. But with some convincing he would not only comply, but also triumph for the cause of the Lord and champion the call of the children of Israel. Upon hearing these lofty words, Gideon began to question the Lord.

"And Gideon said onto him, Oh my Lord, if the Lord be with us, why then is all this befallen us? And where be all his miracles which our fathers told us of, saying, Did not the Lord bring us up out of Egypt? But now the Lord has forsaken us, and delivered us into the hands of the Midianites"
(Judges 6:13)

Wow, and again I say, Wow! What an inflammatory and unsubstantiated accusation. Gideon had the nerve to accuse God for Israel's problems, as though if it were God's doing, or lack of doing. This is not a rare or uncommon accusation levied toward the Lord. He is often the target of all bad things that happen in this world. It seems as if God gets the blame for all things bad, but people give themselves the credit for all things good. Just listen to the comments of some folks.

> *"I just got me a raise on my job. I put all of*
> *my kids through college on a limited budget.*
> *I just paid my home off, no more mortgage.*
> *I just missed having a bad accident on route*
> *490, but I was quick enough to avoid it."*

But when something bad happens, just listen to most folks.

> *"God just took my Grandmother. God let my*
> *best friend lose his leg in a bad accident,*
> *and God allowed me to lose my Job."*

It seems to me that the appropriate application is often misplaced in our society. Our conversation could better go something like this.

> *"Thank God for the time he allowed*
> *Granddad to be with us. I realize it was just*
> *his time to go home to Jesus. Even though I*
> *was laid off as a result of our terrible*
> *economy, I am trusting God for an even*
> *better job in the near future. I have faith in*
> *God and have committed my talents,*
> *experience and resume to Him. God Blessed*

me to put five children through college. We could not have done it without His help. Praise God! Thank God for giving us the strength and wisdom to pay off our home and burn our mortgage."

The Word tells us, *"In all things give thanks for this is the will of God concerning you in Christ Jesus*
(1 Thessalonians 5:18)

Gideon must not have read Job 42. *"In all this Job cursed not the Lord, nor charged him foolishly with his mouth."* The first thing that came to my mind once reading this rebuttal of Job, was that the Angel of the Lord could rightfully have said to Gideon,

"I should be asking you that question- where are all of your miracles? Being that you and your father's house and all of Israel have wholly turned to serving other gods."

Is it possible that while we are tapping and tapping into the arm of God, that He could be saying, "Before you go to searching you should first search out the source of your sins."

Well, that is the way I might have handled it; however, God in His providence had a more methodical way of walking Israel and Gideon through the restoration process.

***

Now the time has come to unveil what I believe to be seven essential steps that will allow you to tap into the veins of God. I feel that in life there must be process. The dictionary describes *process* as being: a series of actions or steps taken in order to achieve a particular end. We must take steps in life. We take steps as babies and go from teetering and wobbling to walking and running. The same procedure is true when it comes to our faith. We start out small, but as we grow, so too, should our faith.

Essential Number 1

Head Toward the Emergency Department

Notice both Gideon and Sister Alexander knew and felt that something in their lives was seriously wrong! Sister Audrey's symptoms were severe headache, pain down left her arm and sudden chest pains. Brother Gideon had issues as well. They included, great fear of the Midianites, planting but not enjoying, having to hide the blessings of the Lord, being the least in his father's house and low self- esteem. Actually, I believe even worse than those symptoms, was remembering being told and possibly reading about the greatness of his people at one time, and not seeing a trace of it in his time. What a tragedy and a reason for a need of immediate remediation from these severe conditions.

In Sister Alexander's case, she did the right thing. She allowed a fellow sister to rush her to the emergency department of a reputable hospital. In Gideon case, Israel's call to heaven's *911* was heard by God Himself. He dispatched the angel of the Lord to go see about an ailing people. The Emergency Department came to Gideon and began to administer help immediately. He proclaimed the Lord, (the best doctor anyone could have), was with Him. He, God, then proclaimed him as a Mighty Man of Valor. Gideon did not know it then, but his healing was being processed from the inside out. You know many times it is our emotional imbalance, or our bitterness, or our un-forgiveness that is really plugging up our blessings from flowing as they should. But don't worry we are in the *Emergency Department* now and we are well on our way to complete healing.

As for you and me, we must know when our situation calls for emergency room help! The Bible says,

"...You have not because you ask not. Ye ask... but ye ask amiss..." (James 4:2-3)

Many times, we wait until the situation is so bad that it requires serious, acute and specialized attention. When we should be living by the old adage 'a stitch in time saves nine.' For those of you too young to understand, that means, back in the day folks used these obsolete items called needles and thread. They would work this lost skill called sewing or stitching. When folks would get a hole in their socks, they would not just throw them out and buy a new pair as they do today. No, no, no, they could not afford to do that. They would simply break out the needle and thread and stitch or sew the hole to mend the socks back together. Well the idea for a 'stitch in time saves nine' is if you sew as soon as you see the hole, beginning one stitch NOW, then you won't have to stitch NINE later down the road.

If we pray now, if we believe now, if we live a clean life now, then we will spend far less time in the emergency room later on!!

Can you just shout Glory on that point? Glory!!!

God wants us to be consistent in our Christian lives, living as unto Him every day.

Well as life goes there may yet be times when we have a need to go to the emergency department (ED). What is our spiritual ED? I think that our ED is when we find ourselves in crisis mode just as Gideon did. Fighting to hold on, trying to believe God, all the while looking at a massive pile of bills, watching a love one slowly die in intensive care or fighting demons in our mind that tell us things that we know to be contrary to the Word and will of God.

"The wicked flee when no man pursueth: but the righteous are bold as a lion."
(Proverbs 28:1)

Through it all, I encourage you to STOP being arrogant, STOP being scary, STOP being stagnant and make up your mind that you are going to fight back.

"Blessed be the Lord my strength, which teaches my hands to war, and my fingers to fight."
Psalms 144:1

Ball up your fists and get ready for a fight! You may not know just how or when, but you must know that with God on your side you cannot lose. You can't be defeated! You must win! You must get to the Emergency Department so that you can tap into God's vein. This is serious! You need that transfusion, like yesterday. Hurry while there is time. Call a prayer partner, call your Pastor, call a prayer line, tell them,

"This is an emergency!"

And by all means, get on your knees and call on Jesus. Ask him for divine direction to one or many of the outlets that I just mentioned to you.

Whatever you do...

MAKE IT TO THE EMERGENCY DEPARTMENT!!

Essential Number 2

Express Your Urgency

After hearing the proclamation of the angel of the Lord, Gideon immediately expressed to Him the sense of urgency that he felt in his spirit. Though misguided and lacking faith, if you will, you have got to give the man credit for expressing that the situation that he saw was dire.

"And Israel was greatly impoverished because of the Midianites; and the children of Israel cried unto the Lord."
(Judges 6:6)

We often are too laid back, casual and placid when it comes to our crisis. I am not saying that we should jump up and down and scream fire every time some little thing goes wrong in our lives. What I am saying is that we should definitely show some vim and vigor when things are messed up, or as the kids say, jacked up.

Once, back in the early eighties, my father-in-law, Pastor Arthur Jones Sr., brother-in-law, Arthur Jones Jr. and myself were moving a refrigerator to his cousin's apartment building. I was the one who got stuck backing up the stairs, holding the top part of this monstrous appliance. Well, as fate would have it, that day one of my size 15 shoes, got stuck on the step and I slipped. When I fell back, that giant fell, full force on my legs. I thought I heard them both snap.

When it fell, I screamed like someone had just stuck me with a giant fork! Boy I screamed like a pig running from the slaughter! When my brother-in-law heard my scream, he jumped up on the fridge, climbed over the top and attempted to help lift the weight off me. When I saw him on top of the fridge, I thought, *well if my legs weren't broken before, they certainly will be now with Junior here climbing on top of me!* Thank God that the only thing that I sustained was a little scrape and nothing more.

My point is that I wouldn't have gotten the help if I had not cried out for it. Let me add here that our cries need to be cries of faith, believing that God will perform His word for us in any giving situation. In fact, we need to walk in the constant belief that, "Whatever, whenever and however I get into a jam, my God is able and also willing to come to my rescue!"

Praise God for His goodness toward us. Why don't you just take a moment right now and send up some praises to store in heaven's bank account! You may need it for a breakthrough, an urgent deliverance, an urgent healing, go ahead and praise him NOW!

Essential Number 3

Link up with the Specialist

You need to know that when you have an acute and specific need, it will take a specialist to deal with your issue. You also need to know that not everyone in your circle may help you to get that specialized treatment. Get to the specialist. I recall a number of years ago, I was going hard in the gym. I was giving it my all and adding a boat load of weight to my workout routine. I had always had a little challenge with my right shoulder, but most times I never felt a thing. This particular day I decided to add plates to my bench-press bar. As I tried to play He Man and jerked the weight up, I felt something strange in my shoulder. I kept working out but the next morning I could barely move.

I called my doctor for a same-day appointment because something was wrong. My doctor sent me to get an MRI. After going through the ten-ton magnet, the people gave me the CD to take to my orthopedic doctor. I figured that instead of waiting to take the CD to the Orthopedist, I would just stop by to see our good friend, Doctor Lisa Harris. She was the head of Internal Medicine at Highland Hospital in Rochester NY. She also ran her own private practice.

Lisa has always been a brain. I thought, *she can just read this CD and give me the news.* The folks at the lab couldn't or wouldn't tell me a thing. They explained that the Orthopedist would have to tell me whether my rotator cuff was torn or not. I thought I could outsmart them by going to see Dr. Harris. I trusted her. She helped me lose over fifty pounds by telling me about the *Advocare* weight loss products. I handed her the CD and asked her to put it in her computer and read it for me. When she did, she just burst into laughter, "Ummmm. Preacher, this is an MRI CD!"

I watched her, "I know that, Doctor friend of mine. I need you to read it for me."

She laughed, "This thing looks to me, the same as it looks to you."

"Hey, you are an award-winning doctor. If anybody can read this thing, I know that you can!"

"Brother Preacher," she continued, "this is not my specialty. You need a Radiologist or an Orthopedist. That is *their* specialty."

Moral of this story: everybody is not qualified to help navigate you through those tough patches in your life. Not everyone has the insight, expertise or concern for you in certain situations. In a medical situation, you will want the best in that field to see about you. Be it a cancer doctor or a brain surgeon, get the best in their field. Likewise, when you are facing a heavy spiritual battle you need to have a real shepherd to help lead you.

Shepherds (Pastors), help guide the flock through all kinds of terrain, rough or tough, cold or hot, dangerous or pleasant. We live in a time when church attendance is at an all-time low. People are choosing rather to stay home and watch church on television or listen to church on the radio. Some even enjoy it on the internet. Media outlets are good for supplemental spiritual meals. However, God never intended for you to survive on a spiritual diet of TV, radio and or internet.

"And I will give you Pastors according to my heart, which shall feed you with knowledge and understanding."
(Jeremiah 3:15)

"Not forsaking the assembling of yourselves together."
(Hebrews 10:25)

Real, live pastors specialize in knowing where your spiritual health lies. Just like a parent can look at their child and know where their head is, their attitude is, their physical health is. A good pastor can look at the sheep and tell where they are and know how to pray and intercede. Going into warfare and feeding and nurturing the sheep back to health.

A good leader can lead you to the vein of God. Please, my friend, don't get caught up in this modern train of thought that says, "I can live saved without being a part of a ministry or having a human Pastor!!!" That's ridiculous thinking. I am a Pastor, but I have a Pastor, always have and always will. Jesus told Peter, *"If you love Me feed my sheep,"* (John 21:17). In other words: *Peter if you love me, love what I love. Love these saints, love the congregation, love the members, and feed them. I have assigned you to be the specialist in their lives. Feed them Peter, as though your very life depended on it.* The thought here is that just like in the animal kingdom, the sheep cannot survive for long without a shepherd; in the church world, sheep don't survive well without a shepherd.

IF YOU SAY THAT YOU ARE SAVED YOU NEED A PASTOR.

Just like a surgeon, a Pastor can lock into your situation and help devise a plan that will help you to defeat the enemy and get started toward reaching the vein of God. You may require a team effort. When people have certain illnesses, they sometimes are assigned a team of doctors, who specialize in certain body parts. Whether the heart, the brain, the kidneys, the blood, the liver or so on. They collaborate together to make the best choices for the patient.

***

I always preach that you need three main folks in your spiritual life: a mentor, a mentee, and peer.

A mentor, hopefully other than the pastor, is someone that has been walking with God longer than you have. They have been invited into your life to be your mentor. They have been given permission to get in your face, jump on your back, and rip your jacket if need be. They ask questions like why weren't you in Bible study? How is your prayer life going? Have you been spending time with your family? You take their toughness because you know that it is given in love.

You also need a mentee. This person is someone that you are bringing along with you on this journey. They have submitted to your mentorship. They allow you to ask questions like, why did you miss Bible study? Have you been praying to God and reading your Word? Have you been spending quality time with your family? You are allowed to get in their face, get on their nerves and jump in their jacket if needs be. This is an attempt to bring them to a place in God's plan where they can find a perpetual flow of His anointing.

And thirdly, you need a peer. This person is a prayer partner, but unlike the two previous persons, this person is a comrade in stocks. You two are traveling the road at about the same pace and possibly the same developmental level. You and your peer are in constant contact and are encouragers to one another. You however, are expected to challenge one another to Godly living and the pursuit of the vein of God for your lives. You may not have the exact same calling, but you are deeply interested in your peer's growth as a Saint and minister of God.

I pray now in Jesus' name, that God will direct you in acquiring these three people in your life. As *iron sharpeneth iron*, you both will do the same in one another lives. Amen!

If you don't currently have a good pastor and a good church home I want to pray for you right now.

> *Father I pray for my friend that is now reading this word and is in need of a pastor and church home. God, I pray that you would direct them to the person and place where they should be. Please do it soon, in Jesus' name. Amen.*

God will also allow others to help as specialists in your life but choose them wisely. Pray this Prayer with me:

> *Father in the name of Jesus, help me to be able to identify those that truly care for me and have my best interest at heart. God, lead me toward spirit-filled specialists that can help guide me toward Your vein.*
>
> *This I pray, in Jesus' name. Amen.*

Essential Number 4

Submit to This Process, Stay the Course, Wait for Change, Insist on Change, Believe God for Change

After seeking the specialist, it is imperative that you follow doctors' orders. So many people lose out on a perfectly good promise, a perfectly good prophetic word, a perfectly good intent of the Lord by not submitting to the process of being blessed. You must understand that there may be a long journey between the calling and the promotion, the calling and the blessing. Sister Alexander was given specific orders to aid the process of getting her blood to flow from her vein to the vials. She had to:

1. Laying still.
2. Squeeze the rubber ball that was given to her in order to pump up her seemingly flat veins.
3. Have faith along with the nurse that the blood would flow.

To me, lying still means to assume the position of humility and submission. When we go to the specialist with the understanding that he knows what he is doing, lying down is certainly a defenseless posture. However, you entered that office with the understanding that he knows how to handle whatever is in his field of expertise and influence. The expert may say run, walk or stand still. It may make absolutely no sense whatsoever. However, submit! God knows what He is doing. In the case of Gideon, God asked Gideon to tear down his father's groves. The groves were a satanic, high, elevated place of worship.

Processing time.

The angel of the Lord told Gideon, "You must do some things in preparation for your nation's miracles. You must make way for the blessings to come your way. There are some major impediments to your deliverance. If you want God to be your God, you must also make Him your Lord." You know, the vast majority of people believe that God and Lord are one and the same. You may recognize Jesus as God, but have you made Him your Lord? Allow me to explain.

> The Apostle Thomas, also known as doubting Thomas, fled as most of the disciples did at the crucifixion of Jesus (Matthew 26:31). However, he heard that Jesus was alive and had been seen around town. Doubting Thomas said to his fellow disciple, "*I will not believe unless I see...*

(John 20:25)." In other words, *"You guys may believe that stuff about Jesus being alive, but to me seeing is believing. And, I will not believe until I actually see for myself."*

Jesus shows up and Thomas proclaims, *"My Lord and my God (John 20:28)."* What he in essence was proclaiming was, *"Not only have I received Him as my sovereign King, high omnipotent and most worshipful Master of my life, He is also my Lord!"* The word 'Lord' means He is my leader. Where He leads me, I will follow. I am lead by His word, His spirit, and by the example that He has left for me. He is my Boss man. David said, *"The Lord is my Shepherd and I shall not want."* He then went on to deal with the duties of a shepherd. The main job of a shepherd is to lead the flock. Along with leading comes the responsibility to feed, protect and have overall care for the flock.

Back to Gideon.

If Gideon wanted to get the prophetic word and miracle for his nation to come to pass, he had to begin to allow the Lord to be his Lord in all matters. God had a humdinger of a challenge for Gideon.

"And it came to pass the same night that the Lord said unto him, 'Take thy father's young bullock of seven years old and throw down the alter of Baal that thy father hath, and cut down the grove that is by it: And build an alter unto the Lord thy God upon the top of this rock."
(Judges 6:25-26)

Wow, what a tall order for a small person. Herein we find some huge impediments:

1. Gideon was the family chump (Judges 6:15).
2. His father, of course, was the family Patriarch.
3. This went against Gideon's personality

But if you intend to be that 'Mighty man' that God spoke of, by faith, your faith has to be elevated to a higher realm. You see, I believe that God gives miracles primarily by His word pushing us to complete an instruction. This is called the 'human element.' For just about every miracle from God, there is a human element or something that must be done by us that moves the hand of God in our favor.

"Moses, what is in your hand?"
Moses answers, "A staff."
"OK, stretch it out..."

The Red Sea divides. The ten lepers walked toward the priest, by faith, and as they walked they were cleansed. The man with the withered hand stretched out his hand by faith and as he did, it was healed. The woman who was broke and ready to have one last meal and die, fed the prophet and was sustained throughout the famine. Another widow went by faith and gathered all of the vessels that she could from her neighbors. She became a rich woman by the actions of her faith. The human element, following instruction, produced her miracle.

We must obey the voice of God in the process of tapping into the flow of His anointing! Grace, praise be unto God. Let's find that vein. Let's seek out the process toward pleasing God. The Bible says that in His presence is fullness of glory. I don't want a fragment of His glory, nor do I want to just experience His glory from time to time. What I'm speaking of is the continuous flow of the presence of God.

Essential Number 5

Expect Some Pain

It seems to me that in the proceeding of anything of substance, there will be some pain, some reconfiguring, and some redefining. Whether it's diamonds, silver, gold or paper, this happens. Either heat, pressure, cutting or natural metamorphosis, this will happen.

Ask gold. It may reply, "Yes, I processed through."

Ask silver. Silver may say, "I was mined, dug out of the hills, mountains and water veins. I was put through the fire and refined. I was cooled, polished and displayed, all to bring out my natural beauty. It was tough, but a part of the process."

Ask paper. Paper may say, "I was cut from the trees, floated down the river, sawed into size, pulverized into pulp, water saturated, bleached, pressed, dried and sized!! It was rough, but it was worth the journey."

Ask the Kangaroo and the answer may be, "One month after conception I had to climb from my mother's birth canal. I was totally blind, as my eyes had not yet developed. Grabbing onto the furry hairs of my mother's abdomen, I inched upward instinctively. Being about the size of a jellybean, this was a long and hairy journey, one which my mother could not hold my hand through or aid me in any way. Once settled into the pouch, I would attach onto the teat and remain there for almost one full year, nursing and growing. This cover, comfort and nutrition would not have been possible if I had not made my initial journey from the birth-canal to the pouch. It was a hilly journey, but part of the process."

Ask the Butterfly. It would say, "I will go through four major stages in my journey of life. This journey can last from one month to a full year depending on what type of butterfly I am.

Stage one: I am laid by my mother as an egg, next to several other eggs onto a leaf. After five days I will hatch from my egg state as a worm like creature.

Stage two: Caterpillar. This stage is sometimes called the larva stage as well. I am now the Caterpillar. Once hatched I have an enormous appetite. I consistently need to eat, and eat, and eat some more. I do it until I've out grown my skin. As a Caterpillar I will shed my old skin and grow new skin. This process is called molting. I will not stay in stage two very long. At this time all I do is eat and grow.

Stage three: Chrysalis (pupa) Stage. This is the stage when I, as a Caterpillar cover myself. I will then protect or hide myself. As a pupa I am often the color of my surroundings. This is the stage when my wings begin to form, although I have reached my full body-size maturity by the time I go into the chrysalis. Although this is called the resting stage, it is not very long.

Stage 4: Butterfly (Imago). At this stage, as a Butterfly, I force my way out of the Chrysalis. It is a tight fit, but I must push my way through without any assistance, the reason being my wings are large, colorful and damp. As I squeeze, I leave behind the fluid that encapsulated me during this incubation period. I am a clumsy flyer at first, but quickly learn to take flight. Once fully developed and venturing out I will find a suitable mate. The Butterfly begins this process of life all over again.

Ask the seasoned saints, and they will tell you that it takes time to save your soul. Salvation is indeed triune. We were saved, we are saved, and we are being saved day by day. It's a processing salvation. If we died today, those of us who are saved will go immediately to heaven. But if we live to see tomorrow, it will be a work in progress.

***

The Doctor tells us to take a deep breath, followed by, "This will be uncomfortable." Well, at least that's what they used to say. I recall about 20 years ago, I got a cyst under my arm that grew to the size of a golf ball, seemingly overnight. I mean this thing just shot up out of nowhere. And let me tell you it huuuurt! Well, I went to my doctor and when he saw it he said, "My goodness Jeff, how did you allow this thing to get so big?"

I said, "Doc., it just snuck up on me!"

He said, "OK Jeff, hold your arm up and get ready, because I need to give you a shot of this numbing substance that is something like Novocain."

I said, "Oh by the way Doc., aren't you supposed to say something like, 'This will be a little uncomfortable, or it's gonna' sting a little?' Not this is gonna' hurt!' Man, you are scaring me!"

He said, "Oh no. We are taught nowadays, to tell folks the truth when it comes to their pain. Oh yeah, *it's going to hurt.*" He was not lying, that process hurt! You should have heard me in there screaming like a second soprano! What a blessing that the windows didn't shatter.

Just like sin, isn't it? Little by little it sneaks up on you and before you know it, it has reached a fever pitch. It is uncomfortable, annoying and is making us sick. If we are not careful, it may even cut the flow of God's anointing right out of our lives. Once this happens, there needs to be trauma in order to right the wrong or to clear the passage.

Have you ever seen a nurse give a shot? Doesn't he or she tap on the needle every time? Well, they are tapping the needle to get the air bubbles out because they know that if a bubble gets in the patient's blood stream, it could make for a bad day! If we get bubbles in the stream of our blessing, that will also make for a bad day.

Bubbles can be our attitude, our negative confession, our erroneous belief system, and even repeating the nay-sayers with whom we hang around. Sometimes we've had a whole life time to build up these negative attributes. Why should we believe that it will all be gone with just the snap of a finger? Even if we receive an instant deliverance, sometimes it will take a painful process to unlearn the things that put us in that bad state in the first place. If we hurt badly enough, we will seek help, hopefully, godly advice. Once we have gotten that advice or counsel, by all means we must use it, apply it, endure it, tough it out! Things will get better.

I recall my Bishop, James R. Wright Sr., a godly man that I love and admire, speaking about an incident. He said that as soon as he came out recovery after having his knee replaced, the nurses had him to get out of bed and walk on his new knee. I mean the same day of the surgery. I remember his mentioning of the intense pain he endured. He was told that this was necessary in order to rehab his knee. According to the doctor you have to move it right away to prevent major problems. You could have the knee and muscles stiffen up so bad only a second surgery could help. He also mentioned how the therapist would come to the house several times per week to exercise and rehabilitate the knee. He would tell the therapist his knee didn't seem to be getting any better, in fact it felt like it was getting worse. The therapist would always give him the same reply, "Bishop Wright it's going to get better, it's going to get better."

May I just encourage you today? When rehabbing our spiritual lives and falling under the total submission of a loving God, it may seem that you are enduring impossible and unbearable pain. But if you just stick with the script and stay the course, I promise you that it's going to get better.

"...endure hardness as a good soldier of Jesus Christ."
(2 Timothy 2:3)

When that nurse slapped Sister Audrey's arm, she meant to traumatize the vein. She needed it to pop up to be available for the drawing. When God traumatizes us, He only wants us to rise up and above our situation. Then we can say as Job said,

"Though He slay me, yet will I trust him." (13:15)

Don't run, don't hide, don't get rid of your spouse, your kids, your church or your job in the middle of your storm. Just hold on, trust God and let him be God!

Psalms 30:5 says,

"For his anger endureth but a moment; in his favor is life (most leave this part out when quoting this scripture, but it's important): *weeping may endure for a night but joy cometh in the morning*!!

Hallelujah!!

In the matter of trauma or injury, the affected area is helped by the plasma rushing to the area to coagulate or pile up in an attempt to protect or surround the injured part. The swelling is sensitive to the touch. Healing is being promoted while the actual wound is covered by these cells. The same is true when we are bruised. We give attention to the area, we favor it, we lean toward, if we cover it, we even put ice on it and immobilize it. The word of God states in Psalms 30:5,

His anger endureth but a moment, in his favor is life. Weeping may endure for a night but joy cometh in the morning.

Whew, powerful!!

It is believed by some Bible scholars that Psalms 30 was written as a result of David being very ill. However, this cannot be verified. We do know that the ancient Jews would use this psalm during the cleaning of their homes. David mentioned that God's anger only endured but a moment. This could have been a reference to the time of God's displeasure with David. In order to have Bathsheba, David ordered her husband, Uriah the Hittite, killed. God certainly punished David. Because of this, there was open shame, rebuke and even the loss of life. However, we serve a great God who gets no pleasure in our discomfort or pain. He does also realize that the discomfort or pain will, if we allow it, take us to a place of the blessing flow of God.

He goes on to say that in His favor is life! To favor is to lean toward or go to. Just as the white blood cells favor the traumatized area of our cut bodies, God favors us with His life-giving flow. We receive blessings and presence only if we allow the traumatic process to go forward. Yes, it may very well come with some agony, angst, and tears. It may seem like the pain will never end. But let me encourage you my friend. It is only a midnight not the whole day. You may ask, "Bishop, just how long will my midnight last?" Let me answer you by saying this: It's not your years, it's your *yield*. There are lessons and virtues and even seasoning that come from our sufferings. I have found that the sooner I get the lesson the sooner my ordeal can be over.

It's not your years, it's your yield. This is a term that God gave me over 25 years ago. It was true way back then, and it is yet true today. As we yield to the lesson or even the chastisement that God allows us to go through, then and only then, will we begin to emerge from the depth of our most trying times and challenges in life. Then we will be able to say like Job said,

"Though he slay me, yet will I trust him. (Job 15:13)

Thank God that our joy will come in the morning. Please know that the night is not literal, but a time frame in which you are going through a trial or season.

It's OK to go through, but it's better to flow through.

While going through your trial, you can find a place of comfort to the point where it just doesn't matter. I call this the 'flow through zone.' I have been on many fast. 1,2,3,or more days and even a 40 day fast. I found out something almost by accident. Your body and mind get to a certain point in the fast where it just doesn't matter. Body pain goes away, the hunger pains disappear, the desire for food no longer plays tricks on your mind. This is the 'flow through zone.' It is as if your mind and body finally get the message that you are in this for the long haul. The body says, "We all must get along because this fella ain't quitting!" Things settle, and you just begin walking in your 'new normal' until your trial is up. I recall coming near the end of my 40 day fast. The closer I got to the end of the fast, the more I wanted to continue the fast. I had become accustomed to not eating and just receiving liquids. It's not that I was masochistic or self-loathing, I just submitted to my desire to please God at the discomfort of my own body.

After a certain amount of time, and submission, your mind, body and soul work as one. When this happens, time, space and situations don't matter nearly as much as they did before. This is a flow of acceptance, flow of anointing, flow of maturity. While this is going on, the Word of God, the Bible, should be first and foremost in your thinking and meditation.

"Thy word have I hid in my heart that I might not sin against thee."
(Psalms 119:11)

Allow me to interject at this point. You must be very careful what you allow in your system during times of trial and sufferings. I like to say don't put anything in front of you that you don't want to get inside of you. Beware of the television, radio, magazines, and even the loose talk that will come your way during these times. The Devil will try his best to poison your walk with God by any way possible. Like the old folks use to say,

"Don't let the devil ride because if he rides he's going to want to drive."

While searching for God's vein, you must be sure that you are allowing Him to flow through you. We are baptized into the body. He in us and we in Him.

Essential Number 6

Cut Off the Negative Flow

Remember at the beginning of the book I mentioned the very confident nurse? Do you also remember that the first trainees in the *yellow shirts* failed to get the vein to pop up in Sister Alexander's arm? Well, from this we realize that the blood was flowing but it needed to be dammed up so that it could be drawn and analyzed. The natural flow of blood had to be disrupted for the wellbeing of Sister Alexander.

There will be times in our lives when the flow of things are just not good enough. Acute action is needed in order to bring about change for the better. If the flow of things in our lives is negative, then we must cut off that flow. I have a saying that goes like this:

If you keep on doing what you've been doing, then you'll keep getting what you've been getting.

It's that simple. When things are not flowing right, there needs to be a disruption in order to get things back on track, or can we say, in the right stream. Some flows are just negative. Let's take the family that has never had a single person to finish high school. Or consider the family whose male members reach the age of 18 or 19 and suffer some life altering event like a prison term, or even worse a trip to the cemetery.

Then there's the family that has teen pregnancies running rampant through its veins. Did you know that nearly 8 out of 10 black and Latino children born today, have fathers who are out of their lives before they are even born? These are generational curses that just need to be cut off. Sometimes in the life of a child, they hear so many negative things that it becomes almost impossible for them to think positively. They hear negative things about life, their living conditions, their education, their fore parents and even themselves. Many of us need to repent to our children and loved ones for creating an environment of negative thinking and speaking. The Bible says,

"A word fitly spoken is like apples of gold in pictures of silver." (Proverbs 25:11)

The Bible also says,

> *"A good man out... of the abundance of the heart his mouth speaketh."* (Luke 6:45)

That means that you didn't just slip and cuss. Cussing was down in you. It just took the right circumstances for the wrong thing to come out. Put it this way, if it was never down in you, it couldn't come out of you.

Tough times and hard trials bring out the best and worst in an individual. Have you ever heard someone that you were convinced was a real quiet person just go O.F.F., or as the kids say, "Go Ham,"? Well what you saw and heard was just the manifestation of what was hidden in their heart. Many people have a quiet riot boiling up on the inside.

I remember when my wife Deborah and I got engaged to be married. Her young sister and brothers-in-law were concerned. They had been around me for months but had never seen me get upset about anything. This bothered them to no end because of course, "Everybody shows some signs of anger when they get ticked off. But this Jeff fella, what gives with his unnatural calm? He's too cool."

What they did not know was that I had years of mastering how to hold my true feelings inside. This taught me how to get by most folks with a smile and a grin. They never knew just how hot I would sometimes get on the inside. This probably came from being the first born, a male, and also trying to be my Mother's protector during times of domestic abuse (that's another book). What I did not know was they were studying me like a book! One day one of them told me, "We figured out how we could tell if you are upset."

I said, "Really, how can y'all tell?"

She said, "Your eyes turn red and your forehead wrinkles." True enough, one day when I was really upset about something (who knows what it was), I ran to the mirror and low and behold, they were right. My eyes were red, and my forehead was wrinkled!

I had to deal with me and cut off the negative flow. Just because I was not ranting and raving, didn't mean that I did not have an anger issue. I did. I needed deliverance. It didn't happen overnight, but through prayer, Bible study and meditation, along with a saturation of soul searching, God helped me to cut off the negative flow. I found out that much of my negative flow came from the disconnect that I had from feeling abandoned by my father.

My mother and father split up when I was six years old. Needless to say, I felt a great deal of rejection and resentment. I also felt an overwhelming need to overachieve. The devil was able to create a negative flow of bad thinking in my mind and a feeling of inadequacy in my spirit. It was not until I came to know who I was in Christ that I was able to begin to tie off the negativity that flowed through my being.

Can I encourage you? You too can and must cut off that negative flow in order to release the full blessings of God. If you find yourself trying to get re-saved in every revival, going from bad relationship to bad relationship, you have a negative flow. If you not only doubt if you are in God, but also if God is in you, there is a negative flow.

Jesus said,

> *"And now also the axe is laid unto the root of the trees."*
> (Luke 3:9)

It is time for you to lay the axe to the root of the negative flow. Bad thinking, self-destructive actions, dream killing words create a negative flow. Even words coming from friends and well-meaning loved ones can stop your connection with the vein of God. Some of them have not yet been set free from self-loathing and family destroying mindsets.

> *"Out of the abundance of the heart the mouth speaketh."*
> (Luke 6:45)

When your ear hear bad things, those things can get in your spirit or your heart. Once they're in your heart, they will flow out of your mouth. Once they leave your mouth, they become the fruit of your lips. Once your lips create fruit, it becomes manifested in your life and the life of your family. Bad thinking will result in bad fruit in your life. It goes, it flows, it kills, it destroys. You must take control. It's not up to God at that point, it's up to you. Jesus said, these and greater things shall YOU do in MY name. The flow must come from your heart to your lips. In order to have good things in your heart you must stop the bad from flowing into your life. Have you noticed that I'm saying the same thing in a lot of different ways?

OK, get it, got it? Good. Let's move on.

Essential Number 7

Let the Blessings Flow

I once heard a story of two former slaves from the deep south who were walking up the freedom trail or Underground Railroad towards the State of New York. Because of Reconstruction, the former slaves had been set free from the oppression of their slave masters. The Emancipation Proclamation had been eloquently given by President Abraham Lincoln, and the fourteenth amendment had been signed and delivered.

While crossing over from Kentucky to Ohio, one of the former slaves suddenly jumped up and hollered to the top of his lungs, "Wheeeeeeeeeeeeeeweeee!!!!!" He scared his fellow traveler so badly, that he ran about thirty yards thinking maybe he had seen a snake, or even worse, a posse coming to drag them back into slavery.

He said to his friend, "Man, what in the world is ailing you? Why did you scream and jump like that?"

His friend answered, "Awww man I'm sorry. I just now realized that I's freeeeeeeeeee!!!"

This may sound comical, but in all seriousness, there are so many of God's people that have been delivered, while not realizing that they are free. They are free from their past, free from the ties that bind them, free from the spirits that torment. Praise the name of Jesus! The Bible says,

"If the Son therefore shall make you free, ye shall be free indeed."
(John 8:36)

To me that means free in your thinking, free in your actions and free from your fears. In addition, you are free to flow in the things of God. To have a free flow in God means that I see it before I see it, I have it before I have it, and I receive it before I receive it. This thinking, and the realization that I have been put into the stream of God's blessings, means I can flow regardless of my situations. Once I have tapped into God, it does not matter what's in my bank account, or what the physician says about my diagnosis, I'm in the flow of God.

***

"Either way, I got Him." Bishop J.O. Patterson, Sr.

I remember when the Late Presiding Bishop of the

Church of God in Christ was diagnosed with cancer. The entire Church was devastated. Bishop Patterson was so beloved, and so revered in the body of Christ. The thought of his passing sent shock waves around the world. We were just not prepared to let him go. Until this day, he remains one of my beloved heroes. He led our church from a small number of 20,000 to a thriving 5 million members worldwide.

I recall seeing him on his weekly broadcast. He had lost a tremendous amount of weight, but he had a fire in his eyes that was indescribable. As he sat on the corner of his desk, he smiled and said, "Saints, my life is in God's hands. Either way this thing goes, I got the devil. If I live, I got him because I will continue to preach the gospel. And if I die I got him because I will be in Heaven with Jesus."

Bishop Patterson had found that flow in God to where it just didn't matter. Yes, he had the faith to be healed, but he also had the faith to know that if he wasn't healed, heaven was his home. The Lord called him home to heaven on December 29th, 1990. I remember that day as though it were yesterday. We drove over 1,000 miles to show our respects at his Home-going services. I remember looking at what seemed to be a little smile on his face and thinking, *This Man of God had an agreement with God. He was in God and God was in him.* He had found that flow and either way it was alright.

Jesus asked the question, "Which is greater, the healing or the forgiveness of sins?" When walking in the flow of God, you are pleased knowing that you have found favor with Him. Yes, you do all of the things that believers do that make them believers. You live for Jesus, you live that sold out life, you treat everybody right. You study, fast and pray. You give your tithes consistently because you want to see the house of the Lord blessed. You also want the reciprocation of God's promises. However, when things don't go your way, and sometimes they won't, that's just life. The Bible says,

"...time and chance happeneth to them all."
(Ecclesiastes 9:11)

It rains on the just as well as the unjust (Matt 5:45). Simply because you are saved does not exempt you from having some unfortunate things happen in your life from time to time. What I'm trying to teach you through this book is that you can reach a place in God that commands the flow of His presence and blessings. By 'blessings' I don't necessarily mean money, houses and lands immediately; I mean that whatever comes I'm able to feel His presence and know that these hard days will soon pass, will soon be over, will soon subside. That's where my confidence lies, my faith presides. The Word of God abides in my life. No matter who dies or who cries, God is yet God!

He is that 'Who God,' the God who is God all by Himself. Without performing, without doing tricks, without amazing us with his abilities, He is God. I tell you, I just want His presence, I want to feel His glory in and about me. Psalms 16:11 sums it up as,

"Thou wilt show me the path of life: in thy presence is fullness of joy; at thy right hand there are pleasures for evermore."

If we could just learn to get in His presence, His blessings would just be a by-product. No father or mother wants to have his or her child seeking his hand all the time, and not his face any other time.

Friends, if we would just learn to get in His face, I mean to intentionally get in His face, do it on purpose, then we could find His flow. I'm talking about having prayer time without asking for one thing. Just prayer time to commune with Him, to be alone with Him, to be in His presence. We then could become like the Hebrew boys who proclaimed, the God that we serve is able to deliver us from your fiery furnace! But if He doesn't...we will not serve you devil...Why? Because we have found the vein of God and we are flowing in His presence.

Finally, you can get to that place called 'there' and I believe that you will if you haven't already. But once you do you can truly say: "I HAVE TAPPED INTO THE VEINS OF GOD."

"And Gideon said unto him, Oh my Lord, if the Lord be with us, why then is all this befallen us?"
(Judges 6:13)

ABOUT THE AUTHOR

Jeffrey L Melvin, the oldest of seven children, was born in Newburgh, New York in 1962 to parents Shirley Jean Jackson and Calvin Lee Melvin.

After moving to Rochester NY with his mother and siblings in 1967, he received Christ as his Lord and Savior at the age of 12 years-old in 1974 at a small church named the Prayer House Church of God by Faith. There he was also baptized and filled with the Holy Spirit.

Bishop Melvin has been favored by the Lord to be blissfully wedded to his wife, Mrs. Deborah Denise Melvin, for over 30 years. The couple has been richly blessed with over a hundred nephews and nieces whom they love as their own.

Bishop Melvin was educated in the Rochester City Schools where he excelled in fine arts and athletics. He later attended Central State University in Wilberforce Ohio where he majored in communications and minored in theatre. After one year of college, he withdrew as he felt a pull in his spirit to become very serious about God and the call on his life. He would later go back to college in 1993 where he earned a Bachelor of Arts degree in Theology with a minor in Christian Counseling. He began his preaching ministry at the age of nineteen under the leadership of his father-in-law, Pastor Arthur W. Jones Sr. His first pastoral assignments were to the *Lackawanna* (later given the name *Potter's House*) *Church of God in Christ* in 1994.

The elevation of Bishop Melvin continued in 2003 when he was assigned, by the late Bishop LeRoy Robert Anderson, to the *Powerhouse Church of God in Christ* in Rochester NY. In 2005 he founded the *Encouragement Centre C.O.G.I.C* in Buffalo NY and a year later became the founding Bishop of the *Rwanda East Africa C.O.G.I.C.*, which is comprised of over sixty churches.

In addition to building the kingdom of God, he also serves as a Special Assistant to Bishop James R Wright Sr., of the New York Western Ecclesiastical First Jurisdiction of the C.O.G.I.C.

Outside of ministry, professionally, Bishop Melvin has a background in radio television and social work and has worked in Christian / Gospel radio ever since 1983. He has been a talk show host on Total Christian Television since 1992. His broadcast both in hosting and preaching have aired around the world.

Bishop Jeffrey L Melvin's favorite saying is, "BE ENCOURAGED".

90078176R00044

Made in the USA
San Bernardino, CA
10 October 2018